The Cat Who Loved Dogs
A True Tale of Love, Loss and Resilience

Sunny Fader

Published in the United States by Booklocker.com, Inc., Port Charlotte, Florida.

Printed in the United States of America on acid-free paper.

Booklocker.com, Inc.
2011

First Edition

The Cat Who Loved Dogs
A True Tale of Love, Loss and Resilience

Sunny Fader

ACKNOWLEDGEMENTS

Without the support of some very special friends, Hillary's story would probably have remained nothing more than a series of mostly happy (and some sad) personal memories. I am eternally grateful to Arlene Hetherington, Valarie Stasik, Pat Holmes and Carol Davies, four very talented women whose encouragement inspired me to commit those memories to paper, and whose keen eyes and editing skills enabled me to turn my manuscript into this book. It is also only fitting that I acknowledge here my thanks to Hillary and Brandy. After all, without them there would never have been a story to tell.

PREFACE

I can't imagine my life without my animals, the dogs and cats that over the years have brought me so much joy and made me a happier, wiser, and I believe better person for having known them. There have been many, each one special in its own way. This is the story of two of those animals: a cunning little cat named Hillary who seemed to understand from birth that her happiness came only in the company of dogs, and her first love, an unwanted, hyperactive young whippet-mix named Brandy. Had my life gone as planned the two would never have met, but then life seldom goes as planned.

The Cat Who Loved Dogs is the story of their friendship. It is a tale of love, loss and resilience, a tale which bears witness to what every cat "owner" knows: that people don't choose their cats; cats choose their people, and—in this case— sometimes their dogs. All the events depicted in the story occurred. All the human and animal characters are real, although in some cases their names have been changed and descriptions altered to protect their privacy.

This book is dedicated to all the cats and dogs who selflessly enrich the lives of their "people." It is also dedicated to those people—those men, women and children who, in opening their hearts and homes to these four legged creatures, reap priceless rewards: companionship, unconditional love, solace when needed, and—if they are really paying attention—sometimes even wisdom.

So please, read on...and enjoy!

Sunny

CHAPTER ONE

The last thing I needed was another cat. I already had two: Tiger, an orange tabby, who bore a closer resemblance to the cowardly lion in the Wizard of Oz than the graceful jungle denizen that had inspired his name, and a clever little beauty, Miss Elizabeth, a grey Abyssinian-mix. All I intended to do, when Leslie telephoned to tell me the kittens had arrived, was go next door to see them.

"I don't know who's more excited, Reisha or Piper," Leslie announced as she let me in the front door. Reisha was Leslie's seven-year-old daughter; Piper was her usually reticent German shepherd rescue. My money was on the dog. I had never seen Piper so animated. She sprinted spiritedly back and forth between us and the bedroom where Reisha was waiting with the new kittens. Apparently displeased with my pace,

1

Piper suddenly swung around behind me and began goosing me down the hallway with a series of inelegant prods.

"Piper, stop that!" Leslie shrieked. Immediately, the dog's tail sagged and she reverted to her usual submissive position at the heels of her mistress. "I just don't know what's gotten into her," Leslie said. "The way she's acting, you'd think she was the one who had the kittens."

I expected Leslie, inveterate animal-lover that she is, to be thrilled with the new litter, but as she opened the bedroom door she seemed more resigned than joyful. When I saw the kittens I knew why. From their markings it was obvious they had been sired by a major source of frustration for my friend: the neighborhood's feline Romeo—an over-sexed, unneutered Siamese. Leslie was convinced the cat, or more precisely its negligent owner, was responsible for our community's burgeoning feral cat population. What she really resented most about the wandering Siamese, however, was the threat it posed to her beloved, but as yet un-spayed Sasha.

There was a reason Leslie had not spayed her new kitten. She believes fervently that unless they are planning to breed their animals, it is the responsibility of all cat owners to spay or neuter their pets. However, Leslie also believes, (rightly or wrongly) that female cats thrive better if they are allowed to go through heat once before being spayed. She knew the risk she was taking and made every effort to keep Sasha indoors. But with a seven-year-old daughter and a rambunctious dog running in and out of the house, the odds of her preventing her cat from encountering the amorous Siamese were always slim at best.

I sympathized with Leslie's frustration, but looking down at the litter there was no doubt in my mind that Sasha's seduction had resulted in the cutest, most irresistible batch of kittens I had ever laid eyes on. My mistake was in picking one of them up. And that is how Hillary came into my life.

CHAPTER TWO

While I was holding the kitten, there was no doubt in my mind that she was meant to be a part of my pack, but once I got home I began having second thoughts. Did I really need the responsibility of another animal? I had just gotten my life back under control after my last pet fiasco. I have a tendency, when impulse prods me to do something I know full well is foolish or impractical, to—under the guise of being rational—weigh the pros and cons of the situation. "It's not the same thing as last time," I told myself. "We're just talking about a kitten here, not another dog."

It's not that I have anything against dogs, mind you. I have one right now. However, at this particular time in my life having a dog just wasn't practical—not for a freelance writer who spent a good deal of her time on the road. That's what I tried to explain to my friend, Connie, that afternoon a little over a year before when she showed up on my doorstep holding a makeshift leash with a quivering young whippet on the other end.

Have you ever had someone in your life with an insatiable passion for rescuing animals? That's my friend, Connie. Miss Elizabeth was one of her rescues. She followed Connie home one day. Connie has this Pied Piper effect on stray animals. Since she already had five rescued cats living with her in a one-bedroom apartment, plus two feral cats she fed outside, she tapped me to give Miss Elizabeth a home, a decision I have never regretted. The whippet, however, was another story.

As soon as I opened the door and saw Connie standing there with the dog, a resolute "NO" formed on my lips. Before I could say anything Connie launched into one of her impassioned pleas for help.

"I need a favor," she said. "I was in Beverly Hills, heading for the Canyon to come home. The traffic was awful. And then I saw this poor dog trapped on the traffic Island. The cars were whizzing by, and she was running back and forth, back and forth, completely spooked. I couldn't just leave her there."

"No, Connie!" I said firmly.

"You know I'd keep her if I could, but with all my cats..."

"No, Connie," I repeated.

"Oh Sunny," she implored, "I'm not asking you to take her permanently. It would just be for a couple days."

"No, Connie," I said again.

"Please, Sunny. I can't take her to the pound. Just look at her. She's already traumatized. You've got a fenced-in yard. She's a sweet dog, really she is. It will just be for a couple of days, I promise—just until I can find her owner."

It was the remark about the pound that got to me. "All right," I said. "But just for a couple of days."

I should have known better. The promise of "just until I find her owner," eventually became "just until I find someone to take her." Months went by and I still had the hyperactive young whippet on my hands. Connie kept assuring me she was looking for someone to take the dog, but given the frequency with which she also told me how happy the animal seemed with me, and what a perfect pair we made, I doubted she was looking very hard.

I believe that once you name an animal, that animal becomes irrevocably yours. And so I refused to give the whippet a name. I referred to her simply as "the dog." However, after three months I realized that this was not working. She needed a name.

I solved my dilemma by borrowing a name for her. The name I borrowed was one my daughter gave a miniature poodle we had rescued some years ago—Brandy. By giving the dog a second-hand name I wouldn't actually be committing myself to a permanent relationship. At least that's what I told myself.

I have to admit that Brandy did turn out to be a sweet dog. Tiger was terrified of her, but she got along well with him, and with Elizabeth, and she was good company for me. The problem was she just didn't fit in with my work schedule—the traveling part. As any animal lover knows, you can leave cats at home for a couple of days. All you have to do is arrange for a friend to come by and feed them and change their litter box.

But a dog—well, a dog has to be walked, a dog has to be talked to, a dog has to have its belly rubbed. Dogs are people-dependent. That meant the expense of a kennel or house-sitter every time I left town.

There was one other problem with Brandy. Like greyhounds, whippets are born to run. And I am not a runner. Walk her? Yes—I could do that. But take her out for a run? Out of the question! So, bursting with pent-up energy, a couple of times a month Brandy would push through the back screen door and run furiously up and down the street, non-stop, for about ten or fifteen minutes. There was no use trying to catch her. My neighbors and I tried that; the more we tried, the more she made a game out of it. I worried about her being hit by a car, but fortunately there wasn't much traffic on the street where I lived. Eventually I learned to just let her get the running out of her system. When she had enough, she would come back to the house and scratch on the door to be let in.

A year went by and Brandy was still part of my little family, in spite of Connie's supposed efforts to find a home for her. Then the Writers Guild of America went on strike, and like all the other screenwriters in town I found myself out of work and on the picket line. Picketing is a tedious chore. To make it more palatable I would take Brandy along. Walking the picket line with me gave her a little exercise and an opportunity to socialize. And, as I said, she was good company.

One afternoon, while we were picketing at CBS, two young men approached us and introduced themselves. "We had to come over," Tim Murphy said. "Your dog is the spitting- image of our Sophie. She was a real sweetheart." Tim's partner, Rob Green, explained that Sophie had contracted a serious kidney problem and they had to put her down. "We really miss her," Rob said.

Brandy immediately took to these young men. I watched as they all three wrestled on the lawn. It was as though they had known each other forever. That's when the idea struck me.

"Look," I said," when they brought her back to me, "Brandy really isn't my dog. She was rescued by my friend. I've just been keeping her until we can find her a home. Would you two be interested in adopting her?"

I knew from the way they smiled at each other that the idea resonated with them. There was some discussion about the two dogs they already had, and whether they would accept Brandy. Tim and Rob debated the problem for a few minutes, but in the end decided that Brandy was so much like the dog they had put down, who had been a part of their pack, that their other two dogs would have no problem with her.

It looked like a win-win situation: In Brandy, Tim and Rob had found an ideal replacement for a much missed dog. For Brandy, the arrangement meant a loving new home, one in which she would find companionship, and more importantly, get the kind of exercise an active dog like her needed. And for me? I had finally found a guilt-free solution to a vexing year-old problem.

The young men and I shook hands and exchanged phone numbers. I handed them the leash, and off they went with their new dog. Brandy's tail was wagging exuberantly. I took that as a good omen.

That had all happened a little over a month ago. Things were now just getting back to normal for me. The strike was

Sonia Fader

finally over, and I was busier than ever trying to catch up on my assignments. It was a relief to be back to just two cats to care for and not have to worry about Brandy any more. So what in the world was I doing taking on responsibility for another animal? "I must be mad," I told myself. I would just call Leslie and tell her to find someone else to take the kitten. But then I would remember how cute she was, and how soft she felt in my hands... and before I knew it, reason went flying out the window.

I went back and forth like this, one day determined not to take the kitten, the next rationalizing that there was no good reason not to take her. She was, after all, a cat—not a dog that would need walking when I was home, and boarding when I was on the road. When Leslie finally called to say the kitten was ready to leave its mother I just happened to be in rationalization mode. And so the kitten came to live with us.

CHAPTER THREE

About her name—almost from the minute I brought her home, the kitten established herself as a champion climber, always seeking out the highest perch in the room. So I decided to call her Hillary, after the world-renowned mountaineer, Sir Edmund Hillary. (I had just read an article about some of his exploits.)

There is something about having a new kitten in the house that lifts the spirit. My new little one's playful antics kept me smiling. A piece of aluminum foil, a cardboard box, a strand of wool—everything triggered her curiosity. She would pounce, leap, attack, retreat, and do a summersault or a back flip. She would scurry, then creep, and finally sprawl with feigned exhaustion. My Hillary was a natural clown.

I have to admit that sometimes, especially when I was working on a tight schedule, Hillary's excessive energy and clowning became problematic—like when she would decide to perform her antics in the middle of the papers on my desk. Aside from the disruptive nature of her activities, there was always the temptation to take time out and play with her, an urge I often found impossible to resist. Still, looking back, it seems to me that the reduction of stress and the sheer pleasure I experienced when I gave into that urge more than compensated for any work time I may have lost.

As for Elizabeth and Tiger, they were not quite as enthusiastic about our new addition as I was, not that I could blame them. Hillary would stalk them, pounce on them as they slept, pester them to play, and intrude into their favorite hiding places. Elizabeth was more tolerant than Tiger. She allowed Hillary to share her favorite nesting place—the out box on my desk. Only occasionally did Miss Elizabeth swat the kitten, and then only when Hillary's pranks became too annoying for her to tolerate.

Tiger, for the most part, ignored Hillary. When she approached him, he would snarl at her and move to another spot. There was one minor confrontation between the perpetually climbing kitten and the tabby, a territorial dispute that led to a brief skirmish between the two. It involved the top of the refrigerator.

Tiger had first sought the safety of the fridge-top when Brandy lived with us. Terrified of the dog, the cat began spending a major part of his day (when he wasn't hiding under the bed or in the closet) perched on top of the kitchen appliance. He continued this practice even after Brandy was gone—that is, until Hillary came along.

Early on the kitten challenged Tiger for the spot. During the short-lived confrontation, Tiger took a few swipes at Hillary, but soon retreated and never again attempted to reclaim the space. Why he succumbed so easily to the demands of a little creature barely half his size I'll never understand.

Well, that's not totally true. Tiger's reaction was completely in character. When he was a kitten his more aggressive litter mates easily intimidated him. I was told that on occasion they had to be removed from their mother so Tiger could get his chance to be suckled. Full grown he was sizable and sturdy, if a bit overweight. He certainly looked like a capable hunter, a cat who would be able to hold his own in a fight. But underneath this deceptive veneer lurked the same timid kitten that went out of his way to avoid confrontation. I'm afraid he didn't inspire much respect, not even from my grown children.

I remember walking into the kitchen one morning in another house I lived in once, out in the countryside, and finding Tiger there with a mouse in his mouth. I was so excited. He finally figured out what he was supposed to do. I called my son, Alan, to tell him the good news.

"Oh Mom," my son laughed, "get real. He probably just opened up his mouth to yawn and the mouse ran in."

Anyway, Hillary claimed the top of the refrigerator and Tiger spent most of the day hiding somewhere. As long as I gave each of my cats what they considered an appropriate part of my time, the three seemed to tolerate each other and all went well. Life moved along without incident—until one afternoon when I received an unexpected phone call that changed everything.

CHAPTER FOUR

It was a typical work day. I was busy at the computer, working on a script, when the phone rang.

"It's Tim Murphy," the voice on the other end of the line said. "I'm sorry to bother you, but I'm calling about Brandy. I'm afraid you are going to have to take her back."

These were not words I wanted to hear. It had taken me over a year to find a suitable home for the dog. Everyone seemed pleased with the arrangement. I never expected to see her again. And now I was being told I would have to take her back? It wasn't fair. Brandy was not supposed to be my dog. Not now, not ever. I was speechless.

"Are you still there, Sunny?"

"Yes, yes, Tim, I'm still here."

For the next ten minutes I listened as Tim related how the well-intended adoption of Brandy had turned into a nightmare. Contrary to what Tim and Rob had hoped, their other two dogs did not readily accept Brandy. Or perhaps the problem was that Brandy was unwilling to accept the position they relegated her to in their pack.

Tim admitted he and his partner had been concerned when their other two dogs kept pushing Brandy aside and wouldn't let her eat until they were finished. "But Brandy seemed to be adjusting," he said, "you know, properly cowering when Rosie disciplined her." Rosie was evidently the alpha dog in the pack. "We thought things were working out," Tim said. "But then last week all hell broke loose."

On this particular evening, Tim told me, Brandy went to eat and, as usual, Rosie growled at her and shoved her away from the dish. Only this time Brandy didn't go. Instead, she viciously attacked Rosie, tearing into her neck with a vise-like grip, and shaking her.

Tim and his partner managed to separate the two, but not quickly enough. Rosie had to be hospitalized and required over forty stiches. There was no doubt in Tim's mind that Brandy would have killed her if they had not been able to stop the fight.

"So you see," he said, "we just can't keep her. We really can't."

I did see, of course, and agreed to take Brandy back, but I had serious misgivings. She was a sweet, friendly dog when she lived with me. What would she be like now? Vicious? Dangerous? And there was Hillary to consider.

I once had a boxer named Tex, a good dog, good with people and other dogs, even some cats—but not kittens. Tex viewed kittens as prey, or perhaps he just played too roughly with them. In either case, his behavior proved fatal for a neighbor's kitten. After Brandy's experience with Tim's dogs how would she react to a kitten?

The telephone rang. It was Tim again. "The vet just called. Rosie is ready to come home, so we were wondering if we could drop Brandy off now."

"Now?"

"It would really be a help."

I would have preferred more time to get ready, but I couldn't refuse them. I called Leslie to see if she would take Hillary for a while, at least until I could see what Brandy was like now. Unfortunately, she wasn't home. Connie, as usual, had a full house. I couldn't think of anyone else who could provide my new kitten with a suitable temporary home.

Before I knew it, Rob and Tim were pulling up outside. I wasn't worried about Tiger or Elizabeth. I knew they would make themselves scarce as soon as the dog came into the house. But Hillary—Hillary had an avid curiosity about anyone who visited and, thanks to Piper, had no fear of dogs. I hustled her into my bedroom for safe keeping.

As soon as I opened the front door, Brandy broke loose from Tim and took a flying leap, grazing my cheek with her tongue. "She recognized the house as soon as we turned the corner," Rob said. Brandy's tail, in fact her whole rear end, was wagging.

"We're really sorry about this," Tim said. "She's a good dog, but it just didn't work out."

I took hold of Brandy's collar and reassured Tim and his partner that I understood. They drove away, and Brandy followed me into the house. Once inside, she plopped down at my feet—actually on my feet—and looked up at me. Her big brown eyes were brimming over with love.

"Well girl," I said, "I guess we're stuck with each other."

I was looking down at Brandy, trying to decide how best to introduce her to Hillary, when Hillary resolved the issue for me. Evidently I had not secured the bedroom door. The kitten came flying into the living room and headed straight for the dog. Brandy popped to her feet. I tried to intercept the cat, but she slipped past me and, before I could stop her, pressed up against Brandy—rubbing against her front leg. Hillary's unexpected appearance startled Brandy, but I saw no signs of aggression. The dog actually seemed pleased to see the kitten. She leaned down and licked the top of Hillary's head.

I was just beginning to relax when Hillary suddenly assumed attack mode. She crouched, bared her claws and sprang at the dog, taking broad swipes. Brandy raised her paw—to strike back, I thought—but then brought it down so gently she barely nudged the kitten. The two of them went at it, back and forth: the cat with all the ferocity she could muster, the dog playfully, with almost maternal gentleness. Finally, worn out from the kitten's antics, Brandy ambled over to the corner and lay down. Hillary followed, and curled up next to her. It was obvious if I was going to have any problems with Brandy, they weren't going to be with Hillary.

The next day I mentioned the instant bonding that had taken place between Brandy and Hillary to Leslie.

"I'm not surprised," she said. "Remember, I told you that when the kittens were born Piper behaved like a midwife?"

"Yes."

"I meant that literally. As each kitten arrived Sasha would lick it clean, but after the third kitten, Piper decided to help her."

"Are you telling me that Piper actually cleaned some of the newborn kittens?"

Leslie nodded. "Two of them. One was Hillary. Poor little thing, she probably hasn't figured out yet that she isn't a dog."

CHAPTER FIVE

From their very first meeting, Hillary and Brandy were inseparable. They played together all day: tag in the yard, hide-and-seek in the house. One of Hillary's favorite games was to jump up on the picnic table in the yard and take swipes at Brandy as the dog ran back and forth under it. They would play like this until the kitten tired of the game. After a brief nap, usually in Brandy's bed, the two of them would be at it again, pursuing some other sport. Hillary kept her hyperactive friend so busy that Brandy never returned to her former troublesome habit of escaping the house and running up and down the street. At night, when it was time to go to sleep, Tiger and Elizabeth inevitably found their way into my bed, but Hillary's bed companion of choice was always Brandy.

About a year after Brandy returned home the house I had been renting was sold. Fortunately, I was able to find another rental in the next block. The location and shape of our space changed, but little else. Hillary and Brandy staked out their territory, Elizabeth and Tiger staked out theirs, and life went on.

As time went by, the kitten matured into a beautiful cat with the stunning markings of her Siamese sire and the graceful lines and sweet disposition of her Lord-knows-what-combination mother, but Hillary never lost her playful kitten-like personality—at least not in her relationship with Brandy.

As much as Brandy enjoyed playing with her feline buddy, she never turned down an opportunity to go for a walk. If we were just going down the street—you know, on one of those quick little walks dog owners take before going out for an evening—Hillary frequently joined us. She would trail close behind, never letting Brandy out of her sight. On our longer walks it would have been too dangerous to let her follow, so I would make sure she was secured in the house before we took off. On these occasions Hillary propped herself on the window sill and watched us go. She was usually still there when we returned.

CHAPTER SIX

It was one of those magnificent fall days in Southern California: The sun was warm, the breeze cool; perfect sweater weather. I had just finished a killer of an assignment. Having been glued to the computer for nearly four weeks, I decided a walk in the hills was just what I needed to recuperate. I donned my hiking shoes, smeared on some sun screen, grabbed my hat and Brandy's leash and, whistling for the dog, headed for the door. Brandy came running. Hillary, as usual, was right behind her.

"Not today, little girl," I told the cat, as the dog and I headed out the door. Destination: Fryman Canyon. Looking back at the house that day I could see Hillary perched on the windowsill, her nose pressed against the pane. If I didn't know better, I would say she was pouting.

One of the things I loved most about living in Studio City, a charming little community in the San Fernando Valley just over the hill from Hollywood, was its proximity to Fryman Canyon. As a confirmed city girl who is, shall we say, directionally challenged, I prefer my encounters with nature close to home, and in small doses. Fryman Canyon fits that bill. It offers a pleasant ninety-minute hike on a fairly steep trail that rises above the city through an unspoiled wilderness area, but never takes the hiker totally out of sight of civilization. Even I could not get lost there.

Normally I would drive to the park, but it was such a lovely day and I had no work to rush back to, so I decided to walk to the beginning of the trail. It was roughly a forty-five minute trek from my house down Ventura Boulevard and up Laurel Canyon.

Brandy did a pretty good job of heeling until we reached the entrance to the trail where, with the promise of freedom just moments away, she briskly took over the lead. She was impatient to get to the open field on top of the ridge where she knew I would remove her leash and let her run free.

It had taken me months to gain the confidence to do this. I had seen other dog owners use the field to exercise their dogs off-leash, but I kept remembering how impossible it was to get Brandy to come to me when she was doing her sprinting-up-and-down-the-street exercise. When I finally did give it a try, much to my delight she came back immediately. I suspect I had Tim and Rob to thank for this. After a couple of successful test runs, I incorporated the off-leash routine into all our visits to Fryman Canyon.

The paved part of the trail rises under a canopy of oak and eucalyptus trees for a short distance, then makes a sharp turn and becomes a dirt path. It was mid-afternoon. The lunchtime hikers were long gone and the after-work hikers and dog walkers had not yet arrived. Brandy and I pretty much had the trail to ourselves.

With a gain of just two hundred and seventy feet the climb is not much of a challenge for true hikers, but thanks to my deskbound lifestyle I was not in the best of shape. Between the incline and trying to keep up with Brandy's eager trot, when we reached the top my heart was doing double time. I took a moment to catch my breath. Brandy pranced around me like a race horse waiting for the starter's gun. I unhooked her leash, and off she went—straight for the open field.

I once worked for a film company that produced promotional material for a greyhound race track in Miami. I spent many an afternoon and evening watching the dogs run, but no race at that track thrilled me as much as watching Brandy that day. She darted across the field, turned on a dime, and raced back to the other side...again and again, with the grace and speed of a champion greyhound. But more than her speed and grace, what I remember most about that afternoon was the sense of sheer joy that emanated from my champion as she sprinted around her self-made track—a free spirit completely present in her moment of unrestrained freedom.

Then, in a flash, she disappeared behind a large boulder. I called to her. A minute passed—two—three. I was about to go look for her when she reappeared. My relief was short lived, however. As she ran towards me I could see something was not right: her gate was unsteady, she seemed off balance, and she was whimpering.

When she reached me I noticed the swelling just above her nose, slight, but enough to distort the shape of her eyes. My first thought was that her insatiable curiosity had finally gotten her into trouble. She had probably stuck her nose in the wrong place and had been scratched or stung by some angry animal or insect. I immediately snapped on her leash and headed down the hill. Whatever the problem was, I wanted a vet to look at her as soon as possible.

Halfway down the trail I began to panic. The swelling was increasing rapidly and Brandy was having trouble staying on her feet. By the time I reached the entrance to the park her legs were buckling. She could no longer stand.

I looked around for help. There was no one in sight. Having no other choice, I picked Brandy up—forty pounds of deadweight; a formidable challenge for a five foot, one hundred-and-twenty pound woman. As I tried to balance my unwieldy load I cursed myself for not having driven, and headed for home, walking as quickly as I could with my burden.

In hindsight, I should have flagged down a car, but I was in panic mode and not thinking clearly. How I made it home I'll never know. Laying Brandy down on the porch, I ran into the house to get the car keys. Hillary scrambled after me, as if she sensed something was wrong. She meowed angrily when I shoved her away from the door as I ran out again.

By the time I reached the Animal Emergency Care Center Brandy was unresponsive and the swelling had distorted her head so badly her eyes looked like two little dots. I picked her up once more and pushed through the front door. Two smocked assistants took her from my arms and told me to have a seat.

It seemed like an eternity, but it was probably only a few minutes before the vet came out. The news was not good: Brandy had been bitten by a rattlesnake. I had not even considered that possibility. I knew there were rattlers in the area, but I had never seen one on the trail.

"Is she in pain?" I asked.

"Some," he said. "But we're taking care of that."

The next question was more difficult to ask. "What—what are her chances?" I could see the answer in his face even before he spoke.

"Well, she's a real fighter," he said. "She's hanging in there. But I'm afraid her chances aren't very good. With rattlesnake bites, time is crucial. For a dog to survive, we need to treat it as soon as possible, before the venom reaches any critical organs. "

I was angry at myself—for letting her off leash, for not taking the car that day, for taking so long to get to the hospital.

"And there is the location of the bite," the vet continued. "It's up high on the nose, almost between her eyes. That means the venom entered close to the brain." He paused to let this information sink in. He never actually put the question into words, but I knew he was waiting for me to make a decision— one I wasn't ready to make.

I tried to sort things out in my mind. The vet had minced no words. He made it clear that the odds were stacked against Brandy. If I decided to buck those odds and tried to save her, there was a good chance I could end up pouring hundreds, maybe thousands of dollars into the effort, and still lose her. Logically, I knew it was time to put an end to her suffering; I knew I should tell the vet to put her down. But I kept thinking about what else he had said—about her being a fighter. She was in the other room right now, fighting—trying to hold on to her life. Brandy wanted to live. How could I not give her that chance?

The vet and I agreed that he would work with her, at least through the night, to see if he could get her through the immediate crisis. He sent me home, promising to call me if there was any change.

CHAPTER SEVEN

Hillary came running the minute I walked through the front door. When she realized Brandy wasn't with me, she hopped up on the windowsill and peered out into the night. She kept that vigil all evening, not even leaving her post to eat.

I checked the hospital before retiring: No change in Brandy's condition. Hillary was still perched on the windowsill when I went to bed, still peering out into the darkness, still waiting for her friend to come home.

The next morning, unable to focus on my work, I went to the hospital to see Brandy. She was still unresponsive, the vet said, but hanging on. He assured me she was not in pain. I sat with her a while, talked to her, told her I loved her and that Hillary and I were anxious for her to come home. There was no sign she knew I was there.

Hillary was clearly disappointed when I returned home again without Brandy. When I tried to pick her up, she ran from me—back to Brandy's bed.

Time hung heavy that day. I straightened up the house, tidied my office, shuffled papers on my desk, tried to get on with life, but it was no use. I wasn't sure just when it had happened, but somehow when I wasn't looking, the dog I had never wanted, the dog I had for so long viewed as a nuisance, had worked her way into my heart. She had become an integral part of my life, and now I couldn't imagine that life without her.

The call came around four o'clock. The voice at the other end of the line was gentle. They had done all they could, but— Brandy was gone.

I thanked the doctor, hung up, and cried. Something brushed against my leg. It was Hillary. At first I thought she somehow knew that Brandy had died, but when she once again took up her vigil at the window I realized she was merely responding to my tears. Hillary still expected Brandy to come home.

I don't remember how long Hillary continued her vigil by the front window, or when she stopped racing to the door every time the bell rang, but in time she did. Somehow she finally understood that her friend would not be coming home. It was as if a great black cloud settled over her. She went into mourning, moping around the house, picking at her food, leaving her favorite treats untouched. I tried to play with her, but if she responded at all, it was with half a heart. She spent most of her time curled up in Brandy's bed. I hadn't put it away yet because of her attachment to it.

Then one afternoon Hillary disappeared.

It was difficult enough losing Brandy; I couldn't lose Hillary, too. I posted flyers with her picture on telephone poles and on market and Laundromat billboards throughout the neighborhood. I delivered flyers to all the veterinarians in the area. I went door-to-door, checking with neighbors in the hope that someone had seen her. I placed ads in the *Los Angeles Times* and all the San Fernando Valley newspapers. I made a pest of myself at the local SPCA.

After a month I finally resigned myself to the fact that Hillary was gone. I could only hope that whoever found her would fall in love with her as I had done, and give her a good home.

CHAPTER EIGHT

About four months after Hillary disappeared I was walking to the store and passed the house where I used to live. I had met the new owners, Janet and Bill Harper, when the house was in escrow, so when I saw Janet in the front yard pruning roses, I stopped to chat. In the course of our conversation Janet mentioned that she and Bill had recently adopted two golden retrievers.

"Congratulations," I said. "They're great dogs."

"Would you like to see them?"

Unable to resist an opportunity to fuss over someone else's puppies, I followed Janet into the house and through to the kitchen. "Aren't they precious," she said gesturing towards the corner. There, napping on a huge dog bed were her two golden retriever pups. They looked to be about six months old.

And tucked in between them, curled up in a little ball, was—Hillary.

Upon hearing Janet's voice the two puppies popped up and, tails wagging, trotted over to greet me. Hillary raised her head, glanced warily in my direction, stretched slowly...and scooted out the doggy door.

"Where did you get that cat?" I asked, as the dogs bounced around me, vying for attention. Janet laughed. "It was the strangest thing," she said. "When we brought the dogs home, I guess it was about four months ago, Bill put in a doggy door. He had no sooner installed the door than this cat came through it. She marched herself right over to the dogs and squeezed in between them. I'm not particularly fond of cats, so we kept putting her out, but she kept coming back in. I swear—she acted just like she lived here."

"Well, as a matter of fact," I said, "she did once." I told Janet the cat's name was Hillary, and how she had been born next door, and had come to live with me when I lived in this house. I told her how Hillary had bonded with Brandy, and how, after Brandy died, Hillary kept waiting for her to come home. "My guess is she finally got tired of waiting, and decided to go look for her."

"Well," Janet said, "she may not have found her Brandy, but she certainly seems to like our dogs. She sleeps with them, plays with them and she even joins in when Bill and I play catch with them." Janet's face clouded over. "I suppose you will want her back," she said. From the disappointment in her voice I suspected that Hillary had managed to cure the woman of her aversion to cats.

"No," I said. "Don't get me wrong. I would love to have her back. I really miss her. But that's not how it works with cats. They pretty much pick their owners—not the other way around. If I took Hillary back to my house she would only come right back here the first chance she got. She came here looking for her dog. While she didn't find her, I'd say she's found two pretty good replacements."

This, of course, dear reader, should have been the end of my story: Cat loves dog, cat loses dog, cat finds new dogs. But, alas, my tale doesn't end here.

CHAPTER NINE

About a year after Hillary took up residence down the street with the Harpers and their retrievers, Miss Elizabeth, Tiger and I moved away from Studio City and settled on an Island off the coast of Seattle in Washington State. From time to time my business brought me back to Los Angeles. On one of those occasions—it must have been about two years after I moved—I decided to visit one of my former neighbors. In the course of our conversation I wondered out loud about how Hillary was getting along. This brought an unexpected burst of laughter from my friend, Gordy.

"What's so funny?" I asked.

"Oh, you don't have to worry about that cat," he said. "Not Hillary, not that little con artist."

"And just what do you mean by that remark?"

"Why don't you pay her a visit and see for yourself."

"Come on, Gordy, you can't just say something like that and leave me hanging."

"I told you," he said. "Go down the street and see for yourself."

Well, I wasn't about to pay an unannounced visit to the Harpers. I barely knew them, and told Gordy so.

"Not the Harpers," he said. "If you want the real dirt on Hillary you need to check next door. That's where she spends most of her time these days."

I assumed Gordy meant where Leslie used to live. Leslie was no longer there. Her landlord had sold her house out from under her too, and she and her entourage had moved to Napa Valley. But if Hillary went back to our old house looking for Brandy, it seemed feasible to me that she might also go looking for Piper, who— if Leslie was to be believed—was a kind of mother figure for Hillary.

"No, no, not <u>that</u> next door," Gordy said. "The other side."

Now I knew Gordy was putting me on. Brenda Harrison lived on the other side of my old house. She had moved in roughly two months before I moved down the street. And the one thing I remembered most about her was how much she disliked cats.

Every once in a while my Elizabeth would wander into Brenda's yard. Brenda was always quick to let me know about it. Oh, she didn't come right out and complain. She was more subtle than that. She would say things like, "Goodness, that grey cat of yours nearly scared my little Joey to death this morning." Joey was her miniature dachshund. Or Brenda would feign concern that my cats might get hit by a car or eaten by a coyote. It was true that coyotes came down from the hills from time to time and were known to make off with a cat or two, but Brenda knew full well that I only let my cats out midday when I was home and the predators were not around. And besides, Elizabeth and Tiger never wandered any farther than my back yard... or on rare occasions, hers.

I never actually heard Brenda say she didn't like cats, but it was obvious when you watched her around Elizabeth or

Tiger—or for that matter—any cat. She would scrunch up her shoulders, purse her lips, and give them the widest berth possible, as if they carried some kind of plague.

"Come on, Gordy, there's no way Brenda Harrison would let Hillary in her house," I said. "The woman clearly hates cats."

"Not anymore," Gordy said.

"Since when?"

"I guess since right before the Harpers got their divorce."

"Wait a minute, the Harpers are divorced?"

"It's a long story, but it was the divorce that triggered the feud."

"What feud?"

"The one between Janet and Brenda. It started when the Harpers both decided to move out of the house while their divorce was pending. Janet was going to take the dogs and go stay with her parents, but she wasn't sure about what to do with Hillary. By this time, Hillary was already spending a good bit of time playing with Brenda's dachshund."

"You're kidding."

"Nope," Gordy said. "So when it came time for Janet to move out, Brenda convinced her to leave Hillary with her. Only then Janet ended up getting the house in her divorce settlement and moved back in, which was fine—until she asked for her cat back."

"Wait a minute."

"Look, just go down and ask Brenda. You can tell her I sent you. You really need to hear the story from her."

From the grin on Gordy's face I was sure he was setting me up, but curiosity got the best of me. I marched down the street and rang Brenda Harrison's bell.

CHAPTER TEN

Brenda cracked open the door. "Well, this is a surprise," she said. I sensed wariness in her voice, as if my turning up unexpectedly on her doorstep presented some kind of threat. Joey peeked out from behind her. Hillary was nowhere in sight.

"I hope I'm not disturbing you," I said, "but I was visiting Gordy, and when I asked him if he knew how Hillary was doing he said I needed to talk to you."

At the mention of Hillary's name Brenda's whole demeanor changed. Her face broke into a broad smile. "Hillary, of course," she said flinging open the door. "You had her when she was a kitten, didn't you? Please, come on in."

I was surprised that Brenda remembered, or even knew I had Hillary then. In the brief time Brenda and I were neighbors Hillary was still a kitten, so I never let her outside. And Brenda and I were not exactly friends. We'd say hello, but never truly engaged in conversation. I had never been in her house, nor she in mine. All this made her sudden unexpected friendliness a bit disconcerting, but I wanted to find out if there was any truth to the wild story Gordy had told me, so I followed her inside.

"Gordy said Hillary is living with you now," I said as Brenda led me into the kitchen.

"Yes. Well, more or less," she said. "I'll just make us a nice cup of tea and tell you all about it."

The kitchen was exactly as I expected it would be: a page out of *Good Housekeeping*, cozy, immaculate, everything in its proper place.

"I'm sorry Hillary's not here right now," Brenda said as she settled me in at the kitchen table. "But it's almost her dinner time. I'm sure she'll be back soon."

"Hopefully before I have to go," I said.

Brenda nodded and offered me an oatmeal cookie. "Help yourself. I made them this morning."

"What did you mean by more or less?" I asked as she filled up the tea kettle.

"It's a bit complicated," she said. "Did Gordy tell you about Janet's divorce?"

"Only that she had gotten one."

Brenda brought some cups to the table, sat down, and filled me in on the details. She told me about how Janet decided to move back to her parents' home temporarily with the dogs, and how she and Janet discussed what Janet should do about Hillary.

"Now you probably know I am not particularly fond of cats," Brenda said, "but Hillary—well she's different. You should see how she and Joey play together. He adores her, and I think the feeling is mutual, because she was spending more and more time in my yard. And it makes sense, doesn't it. I mean, Joey's more her size. Janet's dogs are really sweet, but they are so big. I am always worried that Hillary will get hurt when they start rough-housing with her.

"Anyway, with Hillary being over at my house so much, I have to admit I sort of got attached to her. So when Janet started talking about taking Hillary with her when she moved, admittedly, I wasn't very happy about the idea. It wasn't just that I was going to miss her. I was concerned for Hillary too.

"I told Janet that even if her parents said she could bring Hillary, I didn't think it was a good idea," Brenda said. "Cats don't like change. Moving Hillary twice—first to her parents' house, and then again when she got her own place—would probably really upset the cat. I told Janet that since Hillary and Joey got along so well, I would be happy to take her. I don't think Janet really liked the idea, but she could see it was the best thing for Hillary. So when Janet moved out, Hillary came to live with Joey and me."

Brenda, being Brenda, did not merely take in the displaced cat. She carried her commitment to Hillary to the extreme. She actually gave the cat a room all to herself. Seriously.

"Hillary and Joey are great friends," Brenda explained. "They love playing together. But I noticed that sometimes Hillary would steal off by herself, into my guest room, and curl up on the bed. I mean, all of us need some solitude once in a while, don't we? I hardly ever used the room, so when she came to live with us I decided to fix it up for her. Here let me show you."

Brenda led me down the hall and proudly showed me her redecorated guest room. It was quite a revelation. The double bed was covered with a colorful cat-themed patch work quilt, which I suspect was handmade. In one corner of the room there was a wicker basket filled with cat toys. In the opposite corner Brenda had installed an elaborate climbable scratching post. The walls of the room displayed a variety of cat pictures color coordinated to match the quilt. I was looking at what was undeniably any cat's dream home.

"Hillary is really happy with us," Brenda said. "She's really settled in. So you can see why I was upset when Janet moved back in next door after her divorce and wanted Hillary back."

And that was the beginning of the custody battle for Hillary.

Of course, I only got to hear Brenda's side of the story that afternoon. In her mind, Hillary rightfully belonged to her now. And not just because she had created this "wonderful room" for the cat—although she offered that as strong proof that she had Hillary's best interest at heart. There was also the issue of food.

According to Brenda, she had researched the subject, and was providing Hillary with only the best, most nutritious cat food available, which she sometimes embellished with fresh cooked chicken or shrimp. Janet, on the other hand, according to Brenda, fed the cat whatever cat food was on sale. "So you see, it's not really surprising that Hillary prefers eating at my house," Brenda said.

As it turned out, the matter had not really been resolved. Brenda insisted that Hillary was actually living with her, but admitted that the cat did spend time next door playing with the golden retrievers and that Janet was still referring to Hillary as her cat.

Hillary didn't come back to Brenda's before I had to leave, so I never saw her that day, although I did see pictures of her playing with Joey. Lots of pictures. She was as sleek and beautiful as I remembered her. Before heading back to my hotel, I stopped to say good bye to Gordy.

"Well, it looks like Hillary has everything under control," I said as I was about to leave. "She's found not one replacement for Brandy, but three."

"Four," Gordy said.

"How do you get four? There's Joey and the two golden retrievers."

"And Sergeant. "

"Who the devil is Sergeant?"

"The German shepherd in the house on the other side of Brenda. He belongs to a retired military man, a former Colonel, I think, who moved in several months ago, and seems to be under the impression that Hillary lives with him."

"You've got to be kidding."

"Scouts honor," Gordy said. "Keeps pretty much to himself. I doubt he has given more than a nod to the two ladies in question. But I ran into him a month or so go at the pet shop, and he was buying cat food. I knew he had the shepherd; I saw him walking the dog. When I commented that I didn't know he had a cat too...that's when he told me about Hillary.

"He said he wasn't really a cat person, but one day this cat walked into his house—a Siamese mix of some kind, pretty little thing, and started playing with his dog. He kept putting the cat out, but she kept coming back in, so he let her stay. The dog and she are great friends, he says. She loves to play catch with them. Wanders a lot, he says. Sometimes is gone for days. But she always comes back. 'It's just the darnedest thing,' he says."

"And I take it you didn't disabuse him of his notion that Hillary is his cat," I said when Gordy stopped laughing.

"Why would I do a thing like that, and spoil all Hillary's fun?"

"Good call," I said. "Why indeed?"

FROM SUNNY'S SCRAPBOOK

DURING HILLARY'S REIGN

CPSIA information can be obtained at www.ICGtesting.com
Printed in the USA
LVOW100937081012

301937LV00001B/5/P